INSECT-EATING PLANTS

THE EARTH'S GARDEN

Jason Cooper

Rourke Enterprises, Inc.
Vero Beach, Florida 32964

© 1991 Rourke Enterprises, Inc.

All rights reserved. No part of this book may be reproduced or utilized in any form or by any means, electronic or mechanical including photocopying, recording or by any information storage and retrieval system without permission in writing from the publisher.

PHOTO CREDITS

All Photographs © Lynn M. Stone

LIBRARY OF CONGRESS
Library of Congress Cataloging-in-Publication Data
Cooper, Jason, 1942-
   Insect-eating plants/ by Jason Cooper.
   p. cm. — (The Earth's garden)
   Includes index.
   Summary: An introduction to the remarkable plants with the ability to trap insects and use them for food.
   ISBN 0-86592-624-7
   1. Insect-eating plants—Juvenile literature. [1. Insect-eating plants.]
I. Title. II. Series: Cooper, Jason, 1942-   Earth's garden.
QK917.C66   1991
583'.121—dc20   91-7141
                                      CIP
                                      AC

TABLE OF CONTENTS

Insect-eating Plants	5
Insect-eating Plant Families	6
Homes of Insect-eating Plants	9
Eating Their Prey	11
Sundew	14
Butterwort	16
Venus Flytrap	19
Pitcher Plants	20
Insect-eating Plants and People	22
Glossary	23
Index	24

INSECT-EATING PLANTS

Insect-eating plants don't have claws or sharp teeth, but they do "eat" flesh. That ability makes these plants some of the most interesting and remarkable plants on earth.

Insect-eating plants have bright colors, smells, and flowers to attract insects. Some of the insects are trapped by the plant leaves and become **prey,** or food, for the plants.

Insect-eating plants, also known as **carnivorous** plants, do not chew or swallow prey. Instead, they release juices that break down the insect. Then the plant can soak up part of the animal.

Insect on lip of pitcher plant

INSECT-EATING PLANT FAMILIES

Insect-eating plants live throughout much of the world. About 40 kinds, or **species,** live in North America.

North America's carnivorous plants include six general types: the Venus flytrap, sundews, butterworts, bladderworts, the California pitcher plant, and eastern pitcher plants.

Each type has its own special way to trap insects. And each type has its own look. Some insect-eating plants are tall and straight. Some lie close to the ground.

Roundleaf sundew and northern pitcher plants

HOMES OF INSECT-EATING PLANTS

Insect-eating plants usually live in **wetlands,** like marshes and swamps. A favorite **habitat,** or living place, for these plants is a bog. A bog is the mushy, muddy remains of an old lake that has begun to fill in with dead and dying plants.

One kind of insect-eating plant or another can be found in much of North America. The southeastern United States is rich in insect-eating plants. In some of the grassy areas of the Southeast, pitcher plants grow by the thousands.

Northern pitcher plants in bog

EATING THEIR PREY

In wetlands where insect-eating plants grow, certain **minerals** are scarce. Minerals are important foods for plants.

Over thousands of years, insect-eating plants have developed unusual ways to get the minerals they need. The plants trap insects. The plants take from the insects the minerals they need.

Insect-eating plants don't always have to include insects in their diet. However, they seem to be more healthy when they do.

Insect trapped in bowl of pitcher plant

Yellow trumpet pitcher plants in a Florida wet prairie

White-topped pitcher plants

SUNDEW

Sundew *(Drosera)* leaves sparkle with sticky droplets, as if the plants were always soaked with morning dew. A small insect that steps onto a sundew leaf can't step off. The leaf grabs the insect like glue. Then, tiny spikes on the leaves slowly lock around the insect.

Sundew leaves may be flat on the ground or upright. The largest North American sundew has leaves up to 18 inches long.

Insect trapped in pink sundew

BUTTERWORT

Butterwort *(Pinguicula)* leaves are greasy with liquids that come from the plant. Small insects that crawl or fly onto the leaves become stuck. Slowly, the butterwort's juices make part of the insect into plant food.

Most of the eight species of butterworts in North America have yellow-green leaves. Each plant has one flower blossom in season.

Butterworts live across the northern half of North America and in the Southeast.

Flower of yellow butterwort

VENUS FLYTRAP

Venus flytraps *(Dionaea)* are little plants, not more than four inches across. The flytrap's leaves work much like the shell of a clam.

When an insect enters the open leaf trap, it touches tiny hairs. Movement against the hairs causes the leaves to close together. As the leaf halves begin to shut, guard hairs on the leaf edges keep the insect from escaping.

Venus flytraps are found only in a few places near Wilmington, North Carolina.

Venus flytrap

PITCHER PLANTS

Pitcher plants are the largest of North America's insect-eating plants. One species grows up to four feet tall.

A pitcher plant's leaves grow to form a tube, or pitcher. Insects that visit the lip of the pitcher often wander or fall into it. Escape is difficult. The pitcher plant has a leafy lid, a pool of water in the pitcher, and tiny, downward-pointing hairs.

The California pitcher plant *(Darlingtonia)* lives only in California and Oregon. Eastern pitcher plants *(Sarracenia)* grow in much of eastern and northern North America.

Red, white-topped, and yellow trumpet pitcher plants

INSECT-EATING PLANTS AND PEOPLE

Even though insect-eating plants don't pounce on insects or chase them, these plants are of great interest. Their ability to trap insects and use them for food makes them very unusual.

Because most insect-eating plants live in places where the ground is squishy, people rarely trample them. But many of their homes have been destroyed to make dry land for people's use. When wetlands are drained, the plants in them die.

Where wetlands are safe, insect-eating plants continue to live their amazing lives.

Glossary

carnivorous (kar NIHV or us) — meat-eating

habitat (HAB uh tat) — the area in which a plant lives

mineral (MIN er ull) — certain elements found in nature

prey (PRAY) — an animal caught and used for food by another animal or living thing

species (SPEE sheez) — within a group of closely related plants, one certain kind, such as a *yellow* pitcher plant

wetland (WET land) — an area in which water collects, such as a marsh, swamp, or bog; land covered by shallow water

INDEX

bladderwort 6
bog 9
butterwort 6, 16
insects 5, 6, 11, 14, 16, 19, 20, 22
insect-eating plants
  flowers of 5
  food of 5, 11, 16, 22
  habitats of 9, 22
  kinds of 6
  leaves of 5, 14, 16, 19, 20
  size of 14, 19, 20
  smell of 5

minerals 11
pitcher plant 6, 9, 20
sundew 6, 14
Venus flytrap 6, 19
wetlands 9, 22
Wilmington, North Carolina 19